Dr. Jekyll and Mr. Hyde

BY
Robert Louis Stevenson

EDITED BY
Philip Page and Marilyn Pettit

ILLUSTRATED BY
Philip Page

Published in association with

Hodder & Stoughton

Orders: please contact Bookpoint Ltd, 130 Milton Park, Abingdon, Oxon OX14 4SB, telephone: (44) 01235 827720, fax: (44) 01235 400454. Lines are open from 9.00 a.m. to 6.00 p.m., Monday to Saturday, with a 24-hour message answering service. You can also order through our website www.hodderheadline.co.uk

British Library Cataloguing in Publication Data
A catalogue record for this title is available from The British Library

ISBN 0 340 87159 8

First published 2003
Impression number   10 9 8 7 6 5 4 3 2
Year   2007 2006 2005 2004

Text Copyright © 2003 Philip Page and Marilyn Pettit
Illustrations Copyright © 2003 by Philip Page

Papers used in this book are natural, renewable and recyclable products. They are made from wood grown in sustainable forests. The logging and manufacturing processes conform to the environmental regulations of the country of origin.

Cover illustration by Dave Smith
Typeset by Fakenham Photosetting Ltd, Fakenham, Norfolk
Printed in Great Britain for Hodder & Stoughton Educational, a division of Hodder Headline, 338 Euston Road, London NW1 3BH by J. W. Arrowsmith Ltd, Bristol

Contents

About the story   iv

Cast of characters   v

Dr. Jekyll and Mr. Hyde   1

About the story

Robert Louis Stevenson wrote many novels. *The Strange Case of Dr. Jekyll and Mr. Hyde* was written while he was recovering from an illness, and on his wife's suggestion he improved on his first draft, proving that even great writers have to rework their texts before they are satisfied! It was first published in 1886.

Many readers think that his novel can be classed as a fantasy; others claim it's a horror; while some believe that it firmly challenges the medical practices of the time. The plot explores moral issues and the way humans are attracted to evil.

It has been filmed a great many times and the names 'Jekyll' and 'Hyde' have become part of the English language!

As you read the story, decide who you think is the most interesting and exciting character. Once you've finished the novel, tell your partner which character you chose. Does your choice tell you something about yourself and your attitude to good and evil?

Cast of characters

Henry Jekyll
A respectable doctor.

Edward Hyde
An evil murderer.

Mr. Utterson
A lawyer.

Hastie Lanyon
A doctor.

Two of Dr. Jekyll's closest friends

Richard Enfield
Utterson's friend.

Poole
Dr. Jekyll's butler.

**Inspector
Newcomen**
A policeman.

Two friends, Mr. Utterson and Mr. Enfield, go for their regular Sunday walk. One remembers a very strange event.

Mr. Utterson the lawyer was lean, long, dusty, dreary and yet somehow lovable. He drank gin when he was alone, and though he enjoyed the theatre, had not crossed the doors of one for twenty years.

His friends were those of his own blood or those whom he had known the longest. Hence the bond that united him to Mr. Richard Enfield, the well-known man about town.

It was reported in their Sunday walks that they said nothing, looked dull.

For all that, the two men counted them the chief jewel of each week.

On one of these rambles their way led them down a bystreet in a busy quarter of London.

The shop fronts stood with an air of invitation, like rows of smiling saleswomen. The street shone out like a fire in a forest; with its freshly painted shutters, well-polished brasses, and general cleanliness.

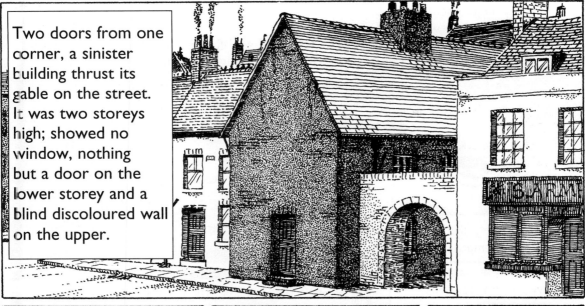

Two doors from one corner, a sinister building thrust its gable on the street. It was two storeys high; showed no window, nothing but a door on the lower storey and a blind discoloured wall on the upper.

The door, with neither bell nor knocker, was blistered. Tramps slouched and struck matches on the panels; children kept shop upon the steps; the schoolboy had tried his knife on the mouldings.

Did you ever **remark** that door? It is connected in my mind with a very odd story.

Indeed? And what was that?

remark – notice

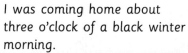
I was coming home about three o'clock of a black winter morning.

Street after street, all the folks asleep, and all empty.

All at once, I saw two figures: a little man stumping along, and a girl of maybe eight or ten running as hard as she was able.

The two ran into one another at the corner ...

... and then came the horrible part; for the man trampled calmly over the child's body and left her screaming on the ground.

It sounds nothing to hear, but it was hellish to see.

I took to my heels, collared my gentleman, and brought him back to the screaming child.

4

The people who had turned out were the girl's own family; and pretty soon the doctor put in his appearance.

I had taken a loathing to my gentleman. So had the child's family. The doctor, every time he looked at my prisoner, turned sick and white with the desire to kill him.

Killing being out of the question, we did the next best.

We told the man we would make such a scandal out of this.

No gentleman but wishes to avoid a scene. Name your figure.

We screwed him up to a hundred pounds for the child's family.

The next thing was to get the money.

He carried us to the door – whipped out a key, went in, and came back with ten pounds in gold and a cheque for the balance ...

... signed with a name that I can't mention, but it was a name very well known and often printed.

A man does not walk into a cellar door at four in the morning and come out of it with another man's cheque.

Set your mind at rest, I will stay with you till the banks open, and cash the cheque myself.

So we all set off, the doctor, the child's father, our friend and myself, passed the rest of the night in my chambers, and the next day went to the bank. The cheque was genuine.

drew – signed

I see you feel as I do. My man was a really damnable man ...

... the person that **drew** the cheque is one of your fellows who do good.

Blackmail, I suppose.

You don't know if the drawer of the cheque lives there?

He lives in some square or other.

You never asked about – the place with the door?

No, sir.

But I have studied the place. There is no other door, and nobody goes in or out of that one but the gentleman of my adventure. There is a chimney generally smoking; so somebody must live there.

I want to ask the name of that man who walked over the child.

Hyde.

What sort of a man is he?

There is something wrong with his appearance; something displeasing. I never saw a man I so disliked. He must be deformed somewhere; although I couldn't specify the point.

I do not ask you the name of the other party because I know it already.

Let us make a bargain never to refer to this again.

After hearing the disturbing story, Mr. Utterson becomes worried about his friend, Dr. Jekyll.

That evening, Mr. Utterson came home and went into his business room. He opened his safe, took from it a document.

Dr. Jekyll's Will

In case of the decease of Henry Jekyll, all his possessions were to pass into the hands of his 'friend Edward Hyde'.

In case of Dr. Jekyll's 'disappearance or unexplained absence for any period exceeding three months', Edward Hyde should step into Henry Jekyll's shoes.

It offended him. Hitherto it was his ignorance of Mr. Hyde; now it was his knowledge.

I thought it was madness, and now I begin to fear it is disgrace.

If anyone knows, it will be Lanyon.

The butler knew and welcomed him.

These two were old friends.

I suppose, Lanyon, you and I must be the two oldest friends Henry Jekyll has.

I see little of him now.

He began to go wrong. Unscientific **balderdash**.

Did you ever come across a Hyde?

Hyde? No. Never heard of him.

balderdash – nonsense

That was the amount of information the lawyer carried back with him.

It was a night of
little ease. He lay
in the darkness.

Mr. Hyde. If he could but set eyes
on him, he might see a reason **for
his friend's preference**.

for ... preference – why Jekyll liked him

Mr. Utterson is determined to find this Mr. Hyde!

From that time, Mr. Utterson began to haunt the door. In the morning before office hours, at noon and at night.

If he be Mr. Hyde, I shall be Mr. Seek.

At last his patience was rewarded. It was a fine dry night; frost in the air; the streets as clean as a ballroom floor; the lamps, unshaken by any wind. By ten o'clock, the shops were closed, the bystreet was very silent. Small sounds carried far.

Mr. Utterson was aware of an odd, light footstep.

Mr. Hyde, I think?

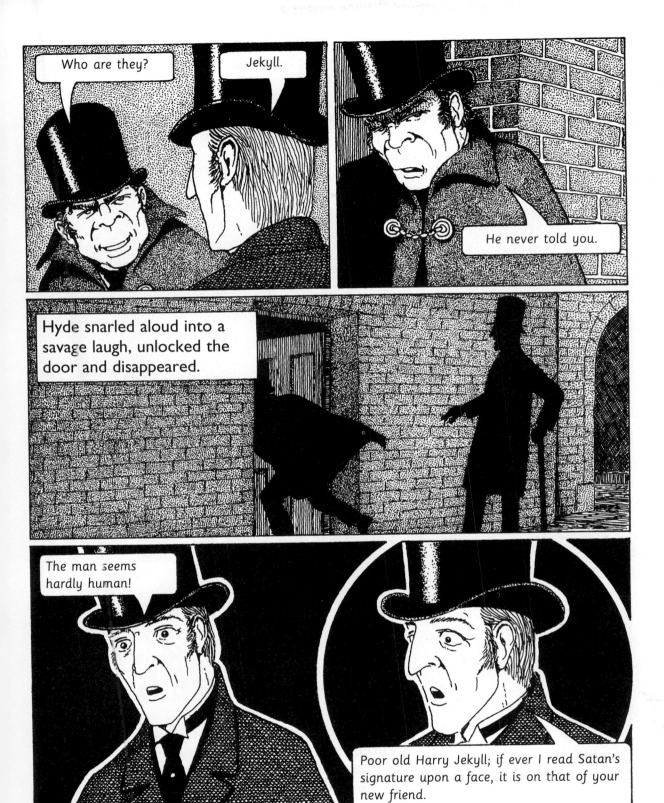

Utterson visits Dr. Jekyll and finds he is not at home. What if Mr. Hyde plans to kill the doctor to inherit the money?

Round the corner, there was a square of ancient houses, for the most part decayed. One house was still occupied. Utterson stopped and knocked.

Is Dr. Jekyll at home, Poole?

I will see, Mr. Utterson. Will you wait here, sir?

Tonight there was a shudder in his blood; he read a menace in the flickering of the firelight.

dissecting room – a room where doctors cut up bodies

Dr. Jekyll was out.

I saw Mr. Hyde go in by the old **dissecting room** door. Is that right, when Dr. Jekyll is from home?

Quite right, sir. Mr. Hyde has a key.

Your master seems to trust that young man.

Yes, sir. We have orders to obey him.

We see very little of him on this side of the house; he mostly comes and goes by the laboratory.

The lawyer set out homeward with a very heavy heart.

Poor Jekyll, **my mind misgives me he is in deep waters!**

This Hyde must have secrets of his own: black secrets, by the look of him.

Things cannot continue as they are. If Hyde suspects the existence of the will, he may grow impatient to inherit. I must put my shoulder to the wheel – if Jekyll will but let me.

my mind ... deep waters! – I fear he's in trouble!

Dr. Jekyll has some friends to dinner and makes Utterson promise to do something he isn't happy about.

A fortnight later, the doctor gave one of his pleasant dinners.

Mr. Utterson remained behind after the others had departed.

I have been wanting to speak to you, Jekyll. You know that will of yours? You know I never approved of it.

Yes, I know that.

Well, I tell you so again. I have been learning something of young Hyde.

I do not care to hear more.

What I heard was abominable.

It can make no change. My position is a very strange one.

You know I am a man to be trusted. Make a clean breast of this in confidence; I can get you out of it.

I believe you; but it is not so bad.

I will tell you one thing: the moment I choose, I can be rid of Mr. Hyde.

I beg of you to let it sleep.

I have a great interest in poor Hyde, and if I am taken away, promise me that you will get his rights for him.

I can't pretend that I shall ever like him.

I only ask you to help him for my sake, when I am no longer here.

I promise.

Hyde murders a man and disappears.

Nearly a year later, a maidservant living alone in a house not far from the river had gone upstairs to bed about eleven.

She sat down under the window.

She became aware of an aged gentleman and another very small gentleman.

She was surprised to recognize Mr. Hyde, who had once visited her master.

He had in his hand a heavy cane. All of a sudden he broke out in a great flame of anger, stamping his foot, and carrying on like a madman. The old gentleman took a step back.

Mr. Hyde clubbed him to the earth, trampling his victim under foot, and hailing down a storm of blows. Bones were **audibly** shattered and the body jumped upon the roadway.

The maid fainted.

It was two o'clock when she came to herself and called for the police.

The stick had broken. A **purse** and a gold watch were found upon the victim; but no **cards** or papers, except a stamped envelope, which bore the name and address of Mr. Utterson.

audibly – noisily
purse – wallet
cards – visiting cards

This was brought to the lawyer the next morning.

He drove to the police station.

I recognise him. I am sorry to say that this is Sir Danvers Carew.

Perhaps you can help us.

He narrated what the maid had seen and showed the broken stick.

Mr. Utterson had already **quailed** at the name of Hyde; but when the stick was laid before him he recognized it for one that he had himself presented many years before to Henry Jekyll.

Is this Mr. Hyde a person of small **stature**?

Small and wicked-looking is what the maid calls him.

I think I can take you to his house.

quailed – flinched
stature – size/build

As the cab drew up before the address, the fog lifted a little and showed him a **dingy** street.

A silvery-haired old woman opened the door. Yes, this was Mr. Hyde's, but he was not at home; he had been in that night very late, but had gone away again in less than an hour.

We wish to see his rooms. This is Inspector Newcomen, of Scotland Yard.

Ah! He is in trouble! What has he done?

Just let me and this gentleman have a look about us.

dingy – dirty-looking

21

Mr. Hyde only used a couple of rooms; but these were furnished with luxury and good taste.

The rooms bore every mark of having been ransacked.

On the hearth lay a pile of ashes, as though many papers had been burned.

The inspector **disinterred** the butt end of a green cheque book; the other half of the stick was found behind the door.

He must have lost his head, or he would never have left the stick or burned the cheque book.

We have nothing to do but wait for him at the bank, and get out the **handbills**.

This last was not so easy; his family could nowhere be traced; he had never been photographed; the few who could describe him differed. Only on one point, were they agreed; unexpressed deformity.

disinterred – uncovered
handbills – wanted posters

22

Mr. Utterson visits Dr. Jekyll and is given a letter written by Hyde. The handwriting is not that different from the doctor's!

It was late in the afternoon when Mr. Utterson found his way to Dr. Jekyll's door. He was received into a large room.

There sat Dr. Jekyll, looking deadly sick.

You have heard the news?

They were crying it in the square.

Carew was my client, but so are you, and I want to know what I am doing. You have not been mad enough to hide this fellow?

Utterson, I swear to God he will never more be heard of.

I hope you may be right.

It was Hyde who dictated the terms in your will about that disappearance?

The doctor nodded.

He meant to murder you. You have had a fine escape.

I have had a lesson – O God, Utterson, what a lesson I have had!

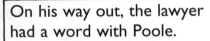

On his way out, the lawyer had a word with Poole.

There was a letter handed in today: what was the messenger like?

Poole was positive nothing had come except by post. This news sent off the visitor with his fears renewed.

Special edition. Shocking murder of an M.P.

He began to cherish a longing for advice.

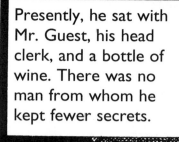

Presently, he sat with Mr. Guest, his head clerk, and a bottle of wine. There was no man from whom he kept fewer secrets.

This is a sad business about Sir Danvers.

Yes, sir. The man, of course, was mad.

I should like to hear your views on that. I have a document here in his handwriting: a murderer's autograph.

No, sir, not mad; but it is an odd hand.

Is that from Dr. Jekyll? Anything private?

Only an invitation to dinner. Why? Do you want to see it?

Thank you.

There's a resemblance; the two hands are in many points identical.

I wouldn't speak of this note.

Jekyll forge for a murderer!

His blood ran cold.

Utterson is concerned that two of his best friends – Jekyll and Lanyon – refuse to meet. He approaches them both but is left even more worried.

Time ran on; thousands of pounds were offered in reward, for the death of Sir Danvers was a public injury; but Mr. Hyde had disappeared as though he had never existed.

Now that the evil influence had been withdrawn, a new life began for Jekyll. He was busy, he did good.

On the 8th January Utterson had dined at the doctor's with a small party.

Lanyon had been there; as in the old days when the trio were inseparable friends.

On the 12th, and again on the 14th, the door was shut against the lawyer.

The doctor saw no one.

On the 15th, he tried again, and was again refused.

He betook himself to Dr. Lanyon's.

He was shocked at the change in the doctor's appearance. He had his death-warrant written upon his face.

I have had a shock and shall never recover. It is a question of weeks.

Jekyll is ill, too. Have you seen him?

I wish to see or hear no more of Doctor Jekyll.

Can't I do anything? We are three very old friends.

Nothing can be done; ask himself.

He will not see me.

I am not surprised at that.

Some day, after I am dead, you may come to learn the right and wrong of this.

As soon as he got home, Utterson wrote to Jekyll, asking the cause of this unhappy break with Lanyon.

The next day brought him a long answer.

...I do not blame our old friend, but I share his view that we must never meet. You must not be surprised if my door is often shut even to you. I have brought on myself a punishment and a danger that I cannot name. I am the chief of sinners. You can do but one thing and that is to respect my silence.

In less than a fortnight Dr. Lanyon was dead. The night after the funeral, Utterson drew out and set before him an envelope.

PRIVATE: for the hands of J. G. Utterson ALONE

He broke the seal. Within was another, likewise sealed.

Not to be opened till the death or disappearance of Dr. Henry Jekyll

Written by the hand of Lanyon, what should it mean?

On one of their walks, Utterson and Enfield see Jekyll at his window. They witness a terrible thing happen to him.

Mr. Utterson was on his usual walk with Mr. Enfield when they came in front of the door.

Well, that story's at an end at least. We shall never see more of Mr. Hyde.

I hope not.

What an ass you must have thought me, not to know that this was a back way to Dr. Jekyll's!

We may step into the court and take a look at the windows. I am uneasy about poor Jekyll.

The middle one of the three windows was half way open; and sitting close beside it, like some **disconsolate** prisoner, Utterson saw Dr. Jekyll.

Jekyll! I trust you are better.

I am very low, Utterson.

You should be out. Come; get your hat and **take a turn** with us.

disconsolate – sad
take a turn – come for a walk

30

I should like to very much; but it is quite impossible.

I would ask you up, but the place is really not fit.

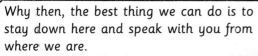

Why then, the best thing we can do is to stay down here and speak with you from where we are.

That is just what I was about to propose.

The words were hardly uttered, before the smile was struck out of his face and succeeded by an expression of terror and despair.

The window was instantly thrust down.

God forgive us!

Poole, the doctor's butler, asks for Utterson's help. He believes Hyde is in Jekyll's house and has murdered the doctor.

Mr. Utterson was sitting by his fireside one evening after dinner, when he was surprised to receive a visit from Poole.

What brings you here? Is the doctor ill?

There's something wrong. He's shut up again in the **cabinet**; and I don't like it.

I can bear it no more.

Try to tell me what it is.

I think there's been foul play. Will you come and see for yourself?

It was a wild, cold night of March, with a pale moon. The wind made talking difficult. The square, when they got there, was all full of wind and dust, and the thin trees in the garden were lashing themselves against the railings.

Is that you, Poole?

It's all right. Open the door.

They're all afraid.

cabinet – small, private room

Poole led the way to the back garden. Utterson followed into the laboratory.

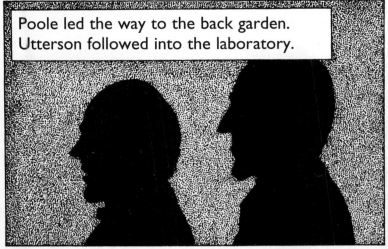

Mr. Utterson, sir, is asking to see you.

Tell him I cannot see anyone.

Was that my master's voice?

It seems changed.

No, sir, master's **made away with**, eight days ago.

Supposing Dr. Jekyll to have been murdered, what could induce the murderer to stay?

made away with – been killed

All this last week him, or it, has been crying night and day for some sort of medicine. I have been sent flying to all the chemists in town.

33

Every time I brought the stuff back, there would be another paper telling me to return it.

Have you any of these papers?

Poole handed a crumpled note.

... their last sample is impure. Dr. J. purchased a large quantity. He now begs them to search, and should any of the same quality be left, to forward it to him at once ... For God's sake, find me some.

This is a strange note.

I've seen him!

I came suddenly into the theatre from the garden. He was at the far end of the room. He looked up when I came in.

Sir, if that was my master, why had he a mask upon his face? Why did he cry out like a rat, and run from me?

They break the door down and find Hyde dead! A letter from Jekyll puzzles Utterson.

There lay the body of a man still twitching.

They turned it on its back ...

... and beheld the face of Edward Hyde.

Life was quite gone. Utterson knew that he was looking on the body of a **self-destroyer**.

We have come too late. Hyde is gone; it only remains for us to find the body of your master.

There were a few dark closets and a spacious cellar. All these they now thoroughly examined. Nowhere was there any trace of Henry Jekyll, dead or alive.

self-destroyer – suicide

He must be buried here.

Or he may have fled.

Utterson turned to examine the door in the street. It was locked; lying near by, they found the key, stained with rust.

It is broken.

This is beyond me.

They mounted the stair in silence, and proceeded more thoroughly to examine the contents of the cabinet.

That is the same drug that I was always bringing him.

This glass has seen some strange things.

What could Jekyll want with it?

On the desk, a large envelope bore, in the doctor's hand, the name of Mr. Utterson. The lawyer unsealed it ...

G. J. Utterson

... and several enclosures fell to the floor.

The first was a will, drawn in the same terms as the one which he had returned six months before; but in place of the name of Edward Hyde, the lawyer read the name of Gabriel John Utterson.

My head goes round; he had no cause to like me; and he has not destroyed this document.

The next paper was a brief note in the doctor's hand and dated at the top.

Poole! He was alive and here this day. He must still be alive; he must have fled.

Why don't you read it, sir?

Because I fear.

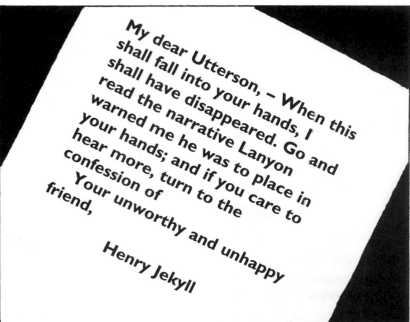

My dear Utterson, — When this shall fall into your hands, I shall have disappeared. Go and read the narrative Lanyon warned me he was to place in your hands; and if you care to hear more, turn to the confession of

Your unworthy and unhappy friend,

Henry Jekyll

There was a third enclosure?

Here, sir.

The lawyer put it in his pocket.

Say nothing of this paper. I must go home and read these documents in quiet. I shall be back before midnight, when we shall send for the police.

Utterson reads Lanyon's account of what happened to Jekyll and Hyde.

On the ninth of January, I received a registered envelope, addressed in the hand of Henry Jekyll. The letter ran . . .

10th December
Dear Lanyon, – Postpone all other engagements for tonight – drive straight to my house, open the glazed press and draw out the fourth drawer from the top. You may know the right drawer by its contents: some powders, a phial and a paper book. This drawer carry back with you to Cavendish Square . . .

. . . at midnight admit a man who will present himself in my name, and place in his hands the drawer. Serve me, my dear Lanyon, and save

Your friend
H. J.

I drove straight to Jekyll's house.

glazed press – glass-fronted cabinet
phial – small glass bottle

I took out the drawer, and returned with it to Cavendish Square. I proceeded to examine its contents.

I found a simple crystalline salt of a white colour. The phial might have been half-full of a blood-red liquor. The book was ordinary and contained a series of dates. Here and there a brief remark: 'double' six times; and once 'total failure!!!'

I dismissed my servants to bed and loaded an old revolver. Twelve o'clock, the knocker sounded very gently on the door.

I found a small man crouching.

Are you come from Dr. Jekyll?

Have you got it? Have you got it?

There it is, sir.

He sprang to it.

Compose yourself.

Have you a glass?

He measured out a few minims of the red tincture and added one of the powders.

The mixture, at first reddish, changed to a dark purple, which faded to a watery green.

And now, Lanyon – behold!

He put the glass to his lips and drank at one gulp.

minims – drops
tincture – mixture

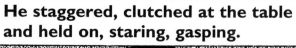
He staggered, clutched at the table and held on, staring, gasping.

His face became suddenly black and the features seemed to melt and alter.

O God!

There before my eyes – pale and shaken – stood Henry Jekyll!

... The creature who crept into my house that night was, on Jekyll's own confession, known by the name of Hyde and hunted in every corner of the land as the murderer of Carew.

HASTIE LANYON.

Utterson now reads Dr. Jekyll's confession which explains what happened when he mixed a drug that changed his personality.

... my scientific studies drew nearer to that truth; that man is not truly one, but truly two. My scientific discoveries had begun to suggest the possibility of a miracle ...

... if each could be housed in separate identities; the unjust might go his way; and the just could walk on his upward path, doing good things. It was the curse of mankind that these polar twins should be continuously struggling ...

... I managed to compound a drug.

polar twins – opposite characteristics
compound – mix

I hesitated long before I put this theory to the test. I knew that I risked death.

But the temptation overcame the alarm.

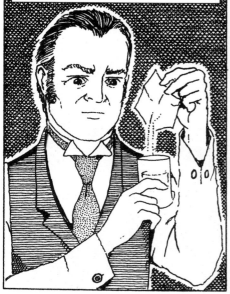

I had long since prepared my tincture; I purchased a large quantity of a particular salt which I knew to be the last ingredient required ...

... and late one accursed night, I watched them boil and smoke together in the glass, and drank the potion.

Racking pangs succeeded: a grinding in the bones, deadly nausea, and horror.

Then I came to myself. I felt younger, lighter, happier.

I knew myself to be more wicked.

I stretched out my hands; and was suddenly aware that I had lost in stature.

There was no mirror in my room. I determined to venture in my new shape as far as my bedroom.

I had lost in stature – I was shorter

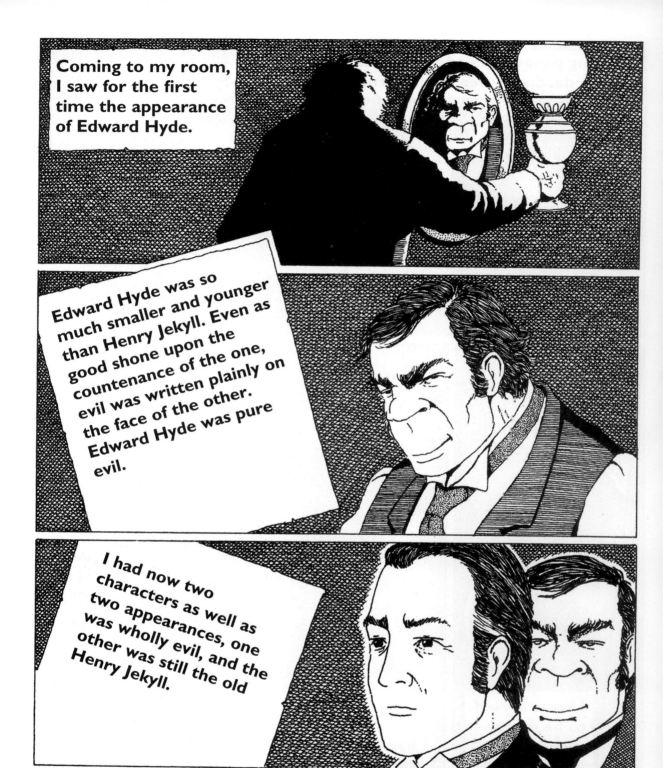

Coming to my room, I saw for the first time the appearance of Edward Hyde.

Edward Hyde was so much smaller and younger than Henry Jekyll. Even as good shone upon the countenance of the one, evil was written plainly on the face of the other. Edward Hyde was pure evil.

I had now two characters as well as two appearances, one was wholly evil, and the other was still the old Henry Jekyll.

countenance – face

I took and furnished that house in Soho, to which Hyde was tracked by the police.

I announced to my servants that a **Mr. Hyde** was to have full liberty and power about my house in the square.

I next drew up that will to which you so much objected, so that if anything befell me in the person of Dr. Jekyll, I could enter on that of Edward Hyde without loss.

Think of it – I did not exist! Give me but a second or two to mix and swallow the draught that I had always ready; and whatever he had done, Edward Hyde would pass away and there would be Henry Jekyll.

draught – drink

The doctor tells Utterson how he began to change from Jekyll to Hyde without the use of the drug. Evil was beginning to take over!

I met with one accident. An act of cruelty to a child aroused against me the anger of a passer by. In order to pacify their resentment, Edward Hyde had to bring them to the door, and pay them in a cheque drawn in the name, of Henry Jekyll ...

... This danger was easily eliminated from the future, by opening an account at another bank in the name of Edward Hyde.

I thought I sat beyond the reach of fate.

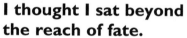

Two months before the murder of Sir Danvers, I had been out for one of my adventures, had returned at a late hour, and woke the next day in bed with odd sensations. My eye fell upon my hand, the hand of Henry Jekyll ...

... It was the hand of Edward Hyde.

I had gone to bed Henry Jekyll, I had awakened Edward Hyde. How was this to be explained? All my drugs were in the cabinet – a long journey down two pairs of stairs.

Ten minutes later, Dr. Jekyll had returned to his own shape.

In the light of that morning's accident, it seemed that I was slowly losing hold of my original and better self, and becoming my second and worse.

I now felt I had to choose.

I chose the better part. I preferred the elderly doctor, surrounded by friends.

I had enjoyed the disguise of Hyde. I neither gave up the house in Soho, nor destroyed the clothes of Edward Hyde. For two months I was true to my determination.

At last, in an hour of moral weakness, I once again swallowed the transforming draught.

My devil had been caged, he came out roaring.

It must have been this that stirred in my soul that impatience with which I listened to my unhappy victim.

The spirit of hell awoke in me and raged.

I mauled the body, tasting delight from every blow.

mauled – battered

I was suddenly struck by a cold thrill of terror. I ran to the house in Soho, and destroyed my papers.

I set out through the lamplit streets.

Hyde compounded the draught and drank it.

Henry Jekyll lifted his clasped hands to God.

I could have screamed aloud; I sought to smother the hideous images and sounds with which my memory swarmed.

I locked the door by which I had so often come and gone, and ground the key under my heel!

The next day, came the news of the crime.

Let Hyde peep out an instant, and the hands of all men would be raised to take and slay him.

Jekyll writes about how frightened he is. He swears he will do good, but things have gone too far. Hyde will not rest!

I resolved to redeem the past. I laboured to relieve suffering.

This innocent life; I enjoyed it completely.

There comes an end to all things.

It was a fine, clear January day, wet under foot where the frost had melted. Regent's Park was full of sweet Spring odours.

I sat in the sun on a bench.

A qualm came over me, nausea and the most deadly shuddering.

I was once more Edward Hyde ...

... hunted, houseless, a known murderer.

redeem – make up for
qualm – faintness/sickness

My drugs were in one of the presses of my cabinet; how was I to reach them? The laboratory door I had closed.

I thought of Lanyon. How should I prevail on the famous physician to rifle the study of Dr. Jekyll? Then I remembered I could write my own hand.

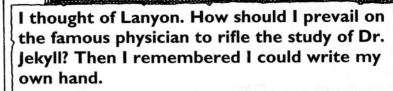

I drove to a hotel in Portland Street.

The attendants led me to a private room, and brought me wherewithal to write.

Hyde composed two important letters, one to Lanyon and one to Poole.

When the night was come, he set forth. He – I cannot say, I. He walked fast, hunted by his fears.

prevail on – persuade
rifle – search

When I came to myself at Lanyon's, the horror of my old friend affected me. The horror of being Hyde racked me.

I came to my own house and got into bed. I awoke in the morning shaken, but I was once more close to my drugs.

I was seized again. It took a double dose to recall me to myself.

If I slept, it was always as Hyde that I awakened. The powers of Hyde seemed to have grown with the sickliness of Jekyll.

The hate that divided them was equal on each side. Jekyll thought of Hyde as something hellish.

The hatred of Hyde for Jekyll, was different . . .

. . . he would play me, scrawling on my books, burning letters and destroying the portrait of my father.

But his love of life is wonderful. When I know how he fears my power to cut him off by suicide, I find it in my heart to pity him.

The salt began to run low. I sent out for a fresh supply, and mixed the draught.

I drank it and it was without efficiency. I am now persuaded that my first supply was impure, and that unknown impurity lent efficacy to the draught.

play – torment
was without efficiency – didn't work
lent . . . draught – made the drug work

Finally, Jekyll knows Hyde is the more powerful. He can only hope that when he changes again, Hyde will die!

This is the last time that Henry Jekyll can think his own thoughts or see his own face. Should the change take me in the act of writing, Hyde will tear it in pieces.

Will Hyde die upon the scaffold? or will he have the courage to release himself at the last moment? God knows; this is my true hour of death, and what is to follow concerns another than myself. Here then, as I lay down the pen and proceed to seal up my confession, I bring the life of that unhappy Henry Jekyll to an end.

THE END